bury it

T0021626

wesleyan poetry

bury it

sam sax

wesleyan university press ▼ *middletown, connecticut*

Wesleyan University Press

Middletown CT 06459

www.wesleyan.edu/wespress

© 2018 Sam Sax

Manufactured in the United States of America

Designed and typeset in Calluna by Eric M. Brooks

Library of Congress Cataloging-in-Publication Data

NAMES: Sax, Sam, author.

TITLE: Bury it / Sam Sax.

DESCRIPTION: Middletown, Connecticut: Wesleyan
    University Press, 2018. Series: Wesleyan poetry

IDENTIFIERS: LCCN 2018008568 (print) |
    LCCN 2018012530 (ebook) | ISBN 9780819577320
    (ebook) | ISBN 9780819577313 (pbk.)

CLASSIFICATION: LCC PS3569.A896 (ebook) |
    LCC PS3569.A896 B87 2018 (print)

DDC 811/.54—dc23

LC record available at https://lccn.loc.gov/2018008568

5 4

National
Endowment
for the Arts
arts.gov

ART WORKS.

*This project is supported in part by an award from the
National Endowment for the Arts.*

for my family

blood & otherwise

פֿאַר װײבער און פֿאַר מאַנסבילן װאָס זײנען אַזױ װי װײבער, דאָס הײסט זײ קענען ניט לערנען

The term "epitaph" itself means
"something to be spoken at a burial or
engraved upon a tomb." When an epitaph
is a poem . . . and appears in a book, we
are aware that we are not reading it in its
proper form: we are reading a reproduction.
The original of the epitaph is the tomb
itself, with its words cut into the stone.

▲ james fenton

I am eager to burn. . . .

▲ essex hemphill

contents

SUSPENSION

bury it

WILL

the fisherman's sneakers trouble the water

he baits his hooks with homophones, cartilage, pheromones

his hooks :   telephones, specula, seraphim

he lowers his line into the dark

         an adrenal needle plunged into the heart

feels something bite below the river

& pulls up boy,

after boy,
after boy,
after boy,
after boy,
after boy,
after boy,
after boy,
after boy,
after boy,
after boy,
after boy,
after boy,
after boy,
after boy,
after boy,

after boy,
after boy,
after boy,
after boy,
after boy,
after boy,
after boy,
after boy,
after boy,
after boy,
after boy,
after boy,
after boy,
after boy,
after boy,
after boy,
after boy,
after boy,
after boy,
after boy,
after boy,
after boy,
after boy,
after boy,
after boy,
after boy,
after boy,
after boy,
after boy,
after boy,
after boy,
after boy,
after boy,
after boy,
after boy,

ROPE

BILDUNGSROMAN

i never wanted to grow up to be anything horrible
as a man. my biggest fear was the hair they said
would snake from my chest, swamp trees
breathing as i ran. i prayed for a different kind
of puberty: skin transforming into floor boards
muscles into cobwebs, growing pains sounding
like an attic groaning under the weight of old
photo albums. as a kid i knew that there was
a car burning above water before this life, i woke
here to find fire scorched my hair clean off
until i shined like glass—my eyes, two acetylene
headlamps. in my family we have a story for this:
my brother holding me in his hairless arms. says

dad it will be a monster   *we should bury it.*

ULTRASOUND

it's not that we're all born
genderless, though we are.
rather, once we were all small
women inside our mothers.
something about science
& sex organs & hormones
& god. no wonder she wept
red negligee when she walked in
on me at ten in her worst dress
spinning before her dead
father's mirror, my eyes made up
into science fictions. felt me
again inside her, my pig thirst
threading her blood & body
mass into another veil i'd wear
& not care for. seeing mother
cry i found myself
into manlier fabrics. when i am
a boy again she tells me
it's not that she hated me fey
rather, that day she swore
she saw the mirror sob. fetal lady,
little daughter, tiny apology.

NEW GOD OF AN ANTIQUE WAR

i only want the world
to end when i'm done
with it

a boy stares into the lake & falls
in love

it's not how you think,
with his own reflection

but rather
the lake

o to be so fluid you can hold
another's shape
& stay the same thing

this story is a horse
beaten into a new name

a french king builds a palace
of mirrors & bankrupts his countrymen

you can't drink glass
without becoming
something else

sure, everyone has heartache
but mine lives
in my body

it moves as i move
it stares back at me

BUENA VISTA PARK 2AM

these men carry
famine in them

eyes
knives

the lamps throw their light
against branches

the branches rake their shadows
across a man's naked back

his back flat as a table
the table set for me

i did not come here hungry
& yet

i eat.

PENTIMENTO

the mass-produced

painting of a field

in winter hanging

above the bed

in this west oakland

motel room starts moving

on its own inside

the faux gold frame.

it begins as always

with whiteness swallowing

the rest of the painting

in its dumb bloodslit

hunger. then as always

a pulse of the backlit

blue veins rising up

like abrasions on a pale

boy's back. followed

by the inevitable red

riven out the snow bank

taking the shape

of a scythe or sieve

or finally a boy or the shape

of a boy growing antlers

or the shape of antlers

wherever his hands

are meant to be now.

but they're impossible

to see in all the movement.

impossible to move

his hands & you have

to wonder how a boy

or the shape of a boy

wound up here

in this unstable field.

if only i knew the history

of art i could give you

more than the color

of the thing. i could tell

exactly what school

this painting's in. i could

use the painter's biography

to make sense of it

his fucked head & terrible

terrible life. i could use

expensive words to make

these bizarre gestures

tenable. i wonder

if every one of these

reprints is moving

in the same fashion?

or is it just this one

staring upside down

at a boy on his back

on a filthy white blanket

while the shape

of a strange man moves

in unspeakable ways

over my body.

STANDARDS

and again the test comes back negative for waterborne parasites
for gonorrhea of the throat and of elsewhere   for white blood cells in the stool

this isn't always true   sometimes it's a phone call from your lover
sometimes it's your computer blinking on with news of what's wrong
          with your body   this time

simple really   how he says the name of a disease
and suddenly you're on your back   staring out the window onto a highway

suddenly a woman enters the room   to wrap a black cuff around your arm
and squeeze until you're no longer sick

to slip a device under your tongue   check if your sweat's accompanied
by the heat it demanded

and aren't we all of elsewhere sometimes   the nowhere places you make yourself
inside the hallowed chambers of the hospital   and inside the man's unsure voice

when he calls and is too scared to name the precise strain of letters
you might share now   what parasite might feed on the topsoil of your groin

what laugh track   what tabernacle unlatched to let all that god in
what bacteria spreading its legs in your throat   as you speak

when the illness is terminal   you drink an eighth of paint thinner
while all the color drains from your face

all those little rocks in your gut turned to buses all those buses full of strange men
each   one degree apart   all going somewhere and gone now

funny how a word can do that   garage the body

what if instead he'd simply called to say   *epithalamium*   or *new car*   or   *sorry*

ESSAY ON CRYING IN PUBLIC

i'm bent over / the sidewalk weeping / outside the public theatre / you stand
above me / horse built from a father's beer cans / you still have that other
man's mouth on you / i can taste it / with the grunt of my hands / it's my fault
/ always is / i say do what you will / + your will is done / so what i was born
drunk + mean with my teeth knocked out / so what my first noise was crying
+ i've been going-strong ever since / that other man has a name / i hate that /
he has a mouth + fixed-gear bike + hiv / + you sat on his couch waiting
for him / to say anything / that you're pretty / or nice / or have nice sneakers
/ then you leapt in his body + lived there a while / maybe brushed your teeth
ate a spoiled piece of fruit / then came back to me / with your house keys
out / the ones i'd cut for you / said you couldn't stop / thinking of me /
how he tasted too sweet / cut flowers in chemical powder / candy souring
in heat / how glad you are to live / here / where everything feels safe / basic
real-estate / my house + bed / a thin sheet of latex / my chest a coffer to store
your futures in / how bad does the news have to be before you get to shoot
the messenger / how can we bury the hatchet / when it always ends up in my back /
when you tell me / he emptied you / like an animal / hide / i'm fine / until
i'm inconsolable / in public + you're offering vacant comfort / *how bad he was
in his body / how much it hurt / you / how you used protection* / + i can't help but think
/ how terrible the name trojan is / in the story / the horse breaks / inside the city
+ war-crazed men spill out / thirsty / for revenge / so what people are staring /
so what we're on our way to the theatre / to see a play where everyone dies /
i don't know why i'm crying either / maybe i can't bare to look at you / covered
in mouths / maybe it's just the sidewalk pulling salt out of my head / maybe
i can't see you now without also seeing you dead

B U R Y

i'm interested in death rituals.

maybe that's a weird thing to say.

when i say interested i mean,

i've compiled a list.

on it are mourning practices

gathered across time & continents.

it's long & oddly comforting

how no one knows a damn thing

about what follows. i won't

share it with you, only say,

evidence suggests neanderthals

were the first hominids to bury

their dead. also, i'll say they

didn't possess a written language,

which points toward interment

as a form of document. the body

is ink in the earth. the grave marker,

a gathering together of text.

the first written languages were

pictorial & marked the movement

of goods between peoples.

i don't know what to do with that

but pretend death's a similar kind

of commerce: face stamped

into a coin, what's left of the body

in the belly of a bird, two lines

that meet to make a man

alive again on paper. i know i know,

ashes to ashes & all that dust

to irreverent dust. i know everyone

i love who's dead didn't actually

become the poem i wrote about them.

their breath a caught fathered

object thrashing in the white space

between letters. contrary to popular

belief elephants don't actually bury

their dead, lacking the necessary

shovels & opposable thumbs. rather

they are known to throw leaves

& dirt upon the deceased & this

is a kind of language. often the tusks

from dead elephants are scrivened

into the shapes of smaller elephants

& sold to travelers who might display

this tragic simulacrum upon

their mantel as a symbol of power

& of passage. when i'm gone, make me again

from my hair. carry me with you

a small book in your pocket.

DRAW

MISSING PERSONS

it's silly
missing anyone
who lives

or maybe
the opposite

you can only
miss the living
in a way
that ferries
marrow up
your spine
in one furious
red curtain

or no
the dead
they're the ones
that open
the asphalt
for ghost-buses
to pour forth from
covered in
ink-black names
scrwld across
the windows

paint-thick names
names so dark
inside you can blink
or be blinded
or die
& be unable to tell
the difference

i miss everyone
all the time

my room's a coffin
with one glass wall

outside
there's a parade
to welcome me

the horns
are so bright
& blood-drunk
you might think
something
was being born

the bullet tore
through my neighbor's brain
like a nail
through a fig

i began
to love him
only once

the ambulances
sang into
the radio-singed stillness

the street after
was empty
as a body
when the soul
climbs out
of the hole
in its head
& becomes
a god

BRIDGES

the truth is that the
bridge is painted
continuously
▲ *Golden Gate Bridge
Tourist Website*

break a glass and try to glue it back
        into a shape that holds water

pilgrims from all over
        throw themselves into the bay's black eyes
           add their names to that dark ledger

when a body hits at these speeds
        water takes
           on the properties of concrete

no good for writing your name in
        for leaving
           anything behind
                a blankness
break a glass

between lip and ocean a figure's
           features blur
             in-between place
in motion
      just limbs and trunk
           just coins and paper money
              lifting up above us

        light straightening
           below water

HYDROPHOBIA

here's how it happened

i drowned the dog
i knew what i was doing
it thrashed
until it didn't

let's start over

i ran the bath
got in myself
watched my dirt change
the color of water

maybe there was no dog
maybe the pills were plants
on my tongue

let me tell you about water

it feeds you as it feeds
without it you die
without you it's fine

once i pulled a burlap sack
from below the surface
of the river

there's a theory
that says if i hadn't opened it
there would not have been a dog inside

inside could have been anything
& it's the act of opening
that caused the dog to be
dead

let's begin again

i ran the bath
called our dog
into the room
she came

there's a theory
that says you don't exist
unless someone calls
& you respond

so my calling called
the dog into existence

i turned on the faucet
but all that came out was dogs

once i was young & holding
onto a kickboard for dear life
as the ocean drugged
my body into water

i called out to the shore
but no one heard me
& for that moment i did not exist

let's begin again

in the beginning there was a bath
& everything living thrashed
toward the surface

the ring around the tub
a mouth that only knows
to swallow

once i was young & holding
onto a man for dear life
take my cock bitch
& it was as if i were listening
through water

let me tell you about water
how it is a grave & vacant lot
how when it gets too hot
it disappears

let me tell you
if he had not opened me
there might not have been a dog
thrashing inside

i'm a thirsty bitch
always drinking water
always starving fishes

let's begin again
in the beginning i knew
what i was doing

then didn't

RISK

how harrowing the paradox of latex. on one hand the paragon of intimacy,
on the other a glove like a father loved more in his absence. my paramour,
my minotaur, my matador flashing his red sword. dear condemnation, i have
read all the commentaries of *raw*, how the forbidden fruit grows less sweet
the more you gorge on it. i've seen the formal debates where two gaping wounds
stand behind podiums + reach into each other's mouths. discourse, its own
form of pleasure. pleasure at its most broken down, a series of shapes.
ethnographies bleed from the ivory tower, the tower made of animal teeth.
the distance between theory + practice is a slick laceration. it's right there
in the name, *unprotected*, to be laid out before the animal in him, to be defenseless
+ deforested. perhaps this is worked out better in myth:

> he pilots my body across a waterbed
> full of drowned squid. in the distance, women
> sing us toward shore.

or perhaps, it's best in images:

> a handful of gravel, the open ground,
> a groveling mouth, a grave half full of water
> with my body not in it yet.

MDMA

my obedient body becomes wild again
obeisant to salt and plastic water bottles
obese cauldron of a boy whose pupils become planets
obstetrician who midwifes serotonin
the kitchen linoleum an obverted dance floor
my skin an obscenity i can't keep my tongue off
so what if this euphoria is only ephemeral
if tomorrow i find the night absconded
        with my smile
if the man i love turns over in his sleep
and becomes a hollowed out gourd
                with a horror mask face
if every object of my intimacy becomes ash
i will still thank each marked and unnamed chemical
        for making oblivion in my blood
dopamine   mephedrone amphetamine
you bring opalescence to the meat
you make the abattoir smell sweet

MEAT

rome's got a broken nose
rome knows the path through the catacombs below paris
rome flowers
rome bath
rome lols & laughs @ once
rome with the same look in all his pictures
rome promises what will become of my body if i let him in
       says he'll play me like a violin
                  while he burns
rome talks big shit
      pretends to be younger than he is
             photoshops color on his lips
       always somewhere "exotic"
rome sends pictures of his dick
      toppled stone column
            caravaggio limp
rome shows up on my doorstep after tracking my phone's gps
rome's very romantic
      basilica filled with spit
        all traffic inside him
emoji's are rome's romance language

he types: wink, angel, diamond
he types: tongue, prayer, pig
          when i don't reply
he types: knife, knife, skull
he types: wolf, gun, toilet

rome throws up small cities on my front steps
rome lifts his skirt & out falls a plague
rome scares the neighbors
                    you can't take rome anywhere
the neighbors say
the neighbors don't care if rome dies
long as flowers

inside my apartment
i let rome inside me

he's fine then   finished
then   fragments

SYNONYMS FOR RAW

uncooked, leading to the spread of bacterium (i.e., salmonella,
toxoplasmosis, avian influenza) [+] uncooked, leading to the spread
of knees (i.e., legs, lips, acropolis) [+] the pulse that breaks your neck [+]
the texture of the carrot skinned with the back of a knife [+] egg
dropped on the floor lapped up by the family dog [+] a statue
of a winged child beaten into a new shape by rain [+] the inflammation
in the throat that follows swallowing [+] honey + cocaine [+] to take
a man how you bard a fowl [+] to take a man + make his blood
your blood [+] to take a man [+] the infection that grows eyes
that open across your torso [+] unrefined sugar [+] allergies to latex [+]
amyl nitrites [+] four letter words (i.e., love, oath, fuck, polish) [+]
to reach inside a person to find nothing there [+] to reach inside
a person + find another hand reaching back

I WANT SO DESPERATELY TO BE FINISHED

WITH DESIRE

after all my labor

                                 pleasure arrives

inelegant as ever

                         secondhand chandelier

onion sound

             the gutter that grunts

back at you when you spit

                                   in its mouth

▲

even with my hand inside him

             he's somewhere else

▲

the shipwreck leaves

         the paired animal bodies

floating   & bloated with salt

▲

everyone drags all their past

         lovers into bed

all their past beds

         & public toilets   & foil pipes

& park benches & deadbolts

         & dead

▲

my hand's inside him
& he's with someone else

gone men breathing
          gone   breath on his neck

▲

the brain is a maniac organ
it puppets me

▲

i follow a man off the subway
into queens   & look up
to see my life has passed

▲

every text message i send
                    is a tongue   pushing through the body
of the phone until it laps
                    at a strained pair of eyes

▲

my man wakes up next to me
                    & recoils
at my hardness
          gathered at his thigh

▲

two primates
          reach between each other's legs
& get to work   one throws his head
          back to stare down god
while the other wants
                    to leave

i press my naked shape
        against aquarium glass
& let the squid swarm
           my deformed organ
they're amazed how it fans out
       like a sibling
brethren & recognition

             every old wound dressed
in drag & daggers

          child of the invert & sodomite
       of the lecher in her leper print
gown of the leper bell
         & its leper sound

my thirst is basic
       easily quenched
water will do

i used to be wild
           unripe fruit

i'd lash myself
to any new mast
while some man stared
          down strange
as i strained
     & galloped terribly
    against his sound

STONE

KADDISH

I grieve. Yet know the
vanity of grief
▲ Robert Hayden

▼

& just like that the first boy i ever kissed is dead / dress lifted
off a mannequin to reveal nothing / man who becomes only
the space he's left / a puncture wound in the upholstery
of my youth / i've arranged his pictures around my bathroom
sink & shaved my face in the dark / trying to make his shape
appear / as it was then / now in my mirror / first boy
i wanted who wanted me back / taught i was worth
such a simple thought as hunger / that lust could be a word
used to describe my own saturnine skin / what is dead
can never rise from bread / what is owed can never be repaid
/ instead this debt / i'm too small to shoulder / maybe this
is my hand's inheritance / to hold / my grief / a pair of gloves
i reach into space / trace the ghost waistband / hear
his voice gasp out from the dark

you came in my mouth in a condom
in the janitor's closet off the hallway
of my freshman dorm in college /
after / i exalted christ as a joke /
christ / & you got small / said jesus
was your personal lord & savior /
the first boy i took in my mouth
had the lord in him / just my luck /
always a half step from salvation /
serotonin spliced with the divine /
the communion wafer that dissolves
above a penitent tongue / the lottery
won with a lost ticket / the barrier when
it would've been better with none

i could afford the flight to new york
i could afford the time off work
i could afford one night in a motel
i could meet a man on my small device there
i could ask him to bring cocaine
i could bring him to my cheap room
i could be cheap with the man there
i could call him your name & he'd bare it
i could watch him break up a line & become you

but to sit in the long pew / among your family
to be judged how i loved
in that company / no i think not
i could not
                    bare it

▼

please

tell
me

how
am
i

supposed
to
go

on

knowing
you

are

[   ]

lust trails the heart around its bone
cage basement / let's say the student
union the night we met was a labyrinth /
let's say you were the minotaur / having
spent more years living as a monster
/ not because i wasn't also a horror show /
taurus-headed boy / desperate for touch
to transform me / let's say i held the sword
& you took me bare inside you / & you were
my first / which means something died
& was reborn / let's say you begged me
to slit your throat & crawl in that slick
wound / let's say i did / let's say i died
/ let's say i never left you /

▼

the official cause of death / according to the autopsy report / was an overdose /
dose from the greek *didonai* to give // to over give / to give too much /
to give over // body opening into the unknown / veil in the skull lifting /
flooding the brain with blood / cocaine comes from the leaves of the coca
plant dried brittle / beaten to dust & dusted with lime // same alkaline stuff
used to quicken the decomposition of flesh // next kerosene in a washing machine
/ next sulphuric acid & mixed again / next bagged & shipped to a processing
plant / potassium permanganate / next shipped across a continent / next stepped
on so much it's almost a dance / that pantheon of chemicals & severed hands /
of gunshot wounds & drug mules carrying plastic in their human stomachs / he took
this inside him / who wouldn't break / him paragon of opportunity / him beauty /
with potential that stretched out metal & pentecostal / blew rails until he was blue
as a eucharist // tachyarrhythmia / cerebral hemorrhaging / hyperthermia // i wonder
what they found / when they cut him / open / wings i bet / i bet they found wings

TOLL

FIRST WILL & TESTAMENT

i look to history to explain & this is my first mistake.
when i say history i mean the stone
half-buried by the roadside has witnessed
more tragedy than a filthy glass of a water. i look to the water
but all i see is dust. i look to the dust & all there is
is history. here's a feather & well of blood
to write the labor movement across the fractal
back of infrastructure. here's a father leaving home
to build railroads with his bare hands. write the laws
that claw the eyes from owls, that build a wall
between the river & the thirsty, that drag families
from one hell into the next. o this house of mine
was built by men & o i, a man sometimes, pass
through its acid chambers & leave out the backdoor
dust. when i say history i mean what lives in us,
i mean the faux gold chain around my neck,
the diseases passed from generation to generation
dating back to a time before christ, i mean any word
traced to its origin is a small child begging for water.

SILENT AUCTION

odysseus strangled a man in the belly
of a wood horse who thought he heard

his wife screaming inside the unconquered
city, the french resistance fed infants

opiate-laced breast milk, josh & i held
each other trembling below the stairs

as my brother & his friends rampaged
through the house, liquor a rampage

in them. silence is what comes
at the end of all our loud suffering

or during it. the film doesn't beg
the organ's accompaniment.

my first time for money i was so quiet
he could hear coins falling inside me

might have mistaken my blood
for a symbol :: crashing.

what i'm arguing for is the impermanence
of beauty—unstuffing the carcass

—when my body is in the ground
disgusting & decomposing,

who will pay to sleep with me then?

WEATHER UNDERGROUND

what was it that drove the weather
underground underground?
what was the switch that flipped back
their hair to show twelve foreheads
crowned with coming bullets?
was it the times, was it the tyrants,
was it the man murdered in his bed
besides his wife, the price of food,
the burning rubber forests, the boys
sent across the world to die?
or was it more like the steady rise
in sea level? a slowly radicalizing shoreline,
the water that comes regardless
of how you build your life raft
from what rhetoric according
to whose religion. arguments over ethics
& tactics braid up into the same
conservative hairdo unless of course
there's a knife to the neck. it's amazing
what a well planted comma can do.
a well placed bomb will change
the meaning of a bus line, a dumpster
fire, police response time, polity, polite
society. the king must always be terrified.
tell me what is it exactly that would
cause you to worm into the dirt
& rise with the flood in order to help
your countrymen breathe. whose hunger
is worthy of your riot today? what does
it take to break civility into actual ass bread?

in college we began to prepare for
the coming devastation, it was always kind
of a joke, still we learned the basics
of farming dead soil, ate each others' semen,
argued over the acquisition of firearms,
built little utopias from our books' imaginations.
apocalypse is too greek a word for
the burning river to come, for the cache
of stolen hair, the camps that have been
& will again spring from the dirt
like rotting turnips. apocalypse means
a veil lifting. the wool from the eyes.
cowardice opening its curtains. comfort
into landmines. it's 70 degrees in february.
my family is under surveillance. the king
must die.

DIASPORA

from desert   to desert

noah crosses   an ocean   + becomes an assault rifle

who of us isn't torn armed   forces cursed to wander the earth in rags

exodus begins: these are the names of the sons of israel

exodus ends   in a shopping mall   sweaters dyed blood-colored

best pray   in new languages

from the cross   to crosswalk   to crosshairs

noah   goes back to the desert   wearing combat fatigues

what's the word   for a man who returns   to a home he's never lived in?

to return   is to reinter   + wreak havoc

this exile into whiteness   witness your child learn

to tongue the slaughter rag   to shed his black hair   for marigolds

WORRY

is a woman
burying bread

beneath her lawn.
praying for summer

to make whole loaves
break in their plastic

shells through dirt
like so many hands.

worry is how i thumb
a groove in the stolen

jewel case in my back
pocket, at tower

records, the man
puts his hands

on me & i'm cooked,
i'm crooked, red

handed, red thumbed.
had enough money

in my pocket
for music

& who really needs
that bad? all my father's

overtime stocked
in our pantry.

all my mother's
edges worried

smooth below
the river of her

boss's hands.
who am i

who steals music
who sells drugs

because i love
how it sounds.

who sold my own
good mouth

for gold. a man
puts his hands

on me &
i'm his & i'm paid.

in the old country
women buried

what little we had
in the dirt & hoped

it would make more
better on earth.

in this country
all food is unzipped

from its plastic
& passes clean through us.

my grandmother's
panic is a relic, is bread

unearthed from
some forgotten dust

bowl still dark
& moldy & whole.

why not eat the hand
that feeds you, i think,

why not eat the arm,
the elbow,

the shoulder? why
not eat the whole

damned body alive.

TREYF

feygele is yiddish for the way i walk into a room.

feygele, the anglicized spelling of angel

fallen into the dark earthen pits of fashion.

feygele from the german vogelein meaning 'little bird.'

little bird, where do you flame from?

where do you bird from little german flame?

little singlet split for entry. little finger slipped

into the mouth staring hard across the bare wet bar.

little bear in his arrogant leather harness, his broad

american faith. carry me with you across the fleshless

threshold how an old woman carries her language

across an ocean so vast, so many fathoms deep

one might imagine all life springing from the wet

slit of its shoreline. sure i've memorized every word

for faggot & nearly all their origins are plural & bound

together with twine. little string corset wrapped

around my brothers' thighs. little horses wild

at the bit to be ridden. little films where the animals

are let out but only at night. sure i've eaten directly

from the hand of a man who taught me the simplest

words, gestures of thirst & begging. sure i was hatched

into a world that expected me to fly straight into power-

lines. but see how hideous hearse-shined my feathers,

see my wings spread like a dead book of legs,

see my brutal beak a seed-thief in the club light.

my first name was flame & i drew moths & mouths alike.

feygela as in son of the first preacher with gills. as in

the flood that began & refused to quench. as in when

i was a child i killed a bird, sparrow i think, with my bare

hands so it wouldn't go on suffering, it was sick.

give me your hands, hold my skull between them

how you'd hold a bag writhing with birds, a pillowcase

thick with lights, two grown boys in gowns howling,

a cold mud village consumed by flames, a cage door

opening, a blade, a blade, ablaze.

ESTATE PLANNING

*for my uncle on the
eve of the first ferguson
demonstration*

city of paint, city of milk paint teeth, city of drink & swallow
city of cholera & wretch medicine, truth & consequence ain't
a city in texas, melancholic city, cocktails ain't just beverages
the velum peeled back by the chemotherapy pill clenched
in my uncle's throat how a hand snatches a bullet mid-air
magic city, the vile imbibed, the acquired carrion stench
the organ transplant list, pharmacist snoring through his morning
barbiturates city, this like all language is the language of death
each letter a suicide penned against its own impermanence
city triumphing over the human breath, city of lesions
on his liver & small intestines, legionnaire city, white blood
cells dressed in their finest immuno regalia, the pills & liquor
that let him weep before his terrified son   i   *don't want*
to die   what came first the disease or the body, the war
or the city or the body, who displaced who from what land
ancient city built on ancient diseases, city growing teeth
& hair inside the empire of his colon, each malignancy
a spire choiring up through the reluctant atmosphere, the air
that carries the brick that splinters the great windows of the mom
& pop gas station, rage made language city, blame the body
for the city that destroys it, blame the city for the body
it destories, for the child left dead in the street for four hours
for the cities that burn after & the cities that burned before,
for the curses torn from the lips like corpse flowers & for
the curtain drawn around the sick man's bed while the surgeon
washes his hands & prepares his knife to open a new door.

CONTROLLED BURN

The air is full of smoke
due to regional wildfires.
. . . Call 911 only if you
see active fire or have
structure fire.
▲ Austin Police
Department

the city smells of smoke though i'm told
the fire's elsewhere. the fire's always elsewhere,
until you can see it, then you're running
toward it or more likely, away. untoward, i know,
the coward in me, who'd never attempt to save
the boutique poodle from the top floor of a burning
house, who'd rather think more in the language
of sacrifice. alas, poor poodle, i knew him, not well.
even noted in my journal years ago, the evening
our telephone pole transformer transformed
into an angry white god outside our apartment,
that there is only one reason human beings
can sleep through the night & it has something
to do with privilege & something to do with pills.
the slow orphic wasp of someone's home aflame
elsewhere, of their photo albums & vinyl melting
into the asphalt, of entire villages reduced to a mouth
pursed around a cigarette. always elsewhere, until
it's not. & finally it's my brother in handcuffs
for possession of a small amount of marijuana
for a blunt half art & half ghost. what unseen
genius to gut a cheap cigar & roll it into scripture.
& later at the station after i paid his meager bail
& retrieved him from deep within the glass cell
his eyes were two burning blankets. on the drive
home he could only shake his head & blink back
ashes for the other men, still imprisoned. who
didn't have a brother to come with money
& a car. if we are to be honest about the nature
of matter, then let us remember when something

burns it's remade as carbon. let us remember
we are carbon if we are anything. that inside
the car's burning engine, the bodies of extinct
fauna alive again. that inside the burning bottle
hurled at the police station, a blindfolded
woman with scales for hands.

IMPOSSIBLE DRAMA

ACT ONE
lights up on a woman. she stares into the audience.
gives birth.

—black out—

ACT TWO
lights up on a boy sitting at a simple table with two glasses
pouring water back and fourth. he does this until the water
spills onto his fingers or onto the table or until
it all has evaporated into the air.

—black out—

ACT THREE
lights up revealing the stage is a huge glass of water. inside
the glass there appears to be nothing but water;
in generations time the single-celled organisms split
and evolved to become visible to the naked eye.

—black out—

ACT FOUR
lights up on two young men sitting on either side of a table.
they pour the contents of empty water glasses back and forth.
all they know how to do is stare at each other. the table grows
legs and leaves, their glasses fill slowly until they spill.

—black out—

ACT FIVE
lights up on a blank stage. the audience's breath troubles
the red curtains in the wings until it appears the whole theatre
is breathing. the moisture from their breath condenses
on the scrim until it begins to drip. it's beautiful.

—black out—

ACT SIX

lights up to show a black river. the river carries silt,
then sediment, then boats, then bodies. so many bodies float
in the black river until there is almost no river left. the banks
of the river are coated in a deep red that grows.

—black out—

ACT SEVEN

lights up on the second young man dressed in radio wires
and electricity. he climbs into a bath and the bath says,

bath: *i am half full and still spilling over.*

the bath says: *i'm sorry.*

says: *give me your cells and in millennia i will make you again.*

—black out—

ACT EIGHT

lights up on a cemetery. only it's not a cemetery.
it's just a hole and it's raining and rain fills the hole
and it's scared the mourners under their umbrellas
when some strange light rises up from the black water.

—black out—

ACT NINE

lights up on a man sitting alone with his water glasses.
the stage is filled with water glasses. the audience too,
beneath their seats or full inside of them. we drink,
everyone drinks.

—black out—

ACT TEN

lights up on stage. it's so bright.
it terrifies.

N A U B A D E

sometimes you pronounce aubade: *obeyed,*
or sponge the face off your own skull, or let go
of a lover's hand how you amputate a septic limb.
perhaps that's too dramatic. but sometimes
he stays until the morning, spoils your toothbrush,
demands scrambled eggs. sometimes he lies
beside you in the dawn after you've wished him
gone, so you pray his breath leaves him,
that some act of grace will extinguish his god
awful noise. god bless the dark, where we all
become something better; he grows wings
or a spine if you want them, you soften
at his touch. the sun is just another instrument
of disillusion. pray instead we live forever
in the dark, grow pale in each other's company,
bathe in the vitamin lamplight. pray we never be
woken from this reverie by a man different
from who we fell asleep beside. better to leave
before the dawn paints its awful fingers across
the room, illuminates and disfigures everything
it tames. remember romance is always a performance,
remember the song heralding the coming light
is not always safe: *i am become death:* remember
his children died in your stomach and across
this great continent you've single-handedly
eaten an entire generation of young musicians.
so you sing from doorframes and it's nothing
like the passion of a moth throwing itself at the blue
flame on a stovetop. no, it is guilt that compels this
song, it is a guilty singing, you sing it every time.

OBJECTOPHILE

everyone knows about the woman who fell in love with the bridge
but no one cares how the bridge felt after.

everyone knows about the poet who leapt from the deck of a ship
but not how the boat lifted & bloated in his wake like a white infant
spread over the bed of a lake.

we leave our objects behind us. we collect our dead's leavings & listen
for their breathing in the soft mouths of gloves. we believe them.

i care too much & still have the dead boy's red sweater. i tongue
the wound. i tender this mule. i unravel quick my flesh debt.

every word an object in my dark wet house. everyone asks after
the living but no one cares how the cotton sobs in my mouth.

i am become warehouse   :   i am destroy speech.

everyone knows the poet fell from the bridge because he jumped.
no one cares there's nothing left for us but his poems

not even a simple plaque drilled into the bridge's throat reads :

> *this is where the man lived*
> *this is where the man broke*
> *this is the man*
> *this is the man stretched*
> *between two cold cities*
> *you are standing*
> *on his back.*

SURVEILLANCE

Jumping off gw
bridge sorry
▲ *Tyler Clementi's last
facebook post*

it's a tragic technology — the body — the camera's aperture —
a mouth — the internet feed — undiscerning — his suicide
— a cry for help — in the forums of a pornography site —
the young man — his violin — was torn — his passion
— a cramped room — a leaden sky — a prank — a crime —
governor said, *i don't know how those two folks are going
to sleep at night* — his thirty-two-year-old man — his music —
his eighteen years — his roommate's camera — embarrassment
never ends — no body has been recovered — the webcam —
aimed at his bed — his tragedy made him a martyr — these
are his lover's trembling hands — charged with invasion —
these are just stories — the september it seemed every gay boy
was dying — beyond words — the camera staring out at me —
convicted of spying — the body of christ — dragged out
of the hudson — the video stream — a person by nature —
the bravery of a thread — his man didn't know tyler's last
name until he read it in the paper — his last words posted —
ten minutes before — he was dead

SUSPENSION

POLITICS OF ELEGY

like anyone i can make a list of the dead

i can make them my dead by making the list

i can write my name then name names below it

i can craft & obfuscate & collapse

i can publish it

i can ask 'who of us is left to tell their story?'

this land of plentitude & pens

this land is my land, the song says, this land is mine

how long have humans buried each other in the earth

how long have we sung names into their absence

how long have we been paid for that singing

every architect expects people to inhabit their buildings

every poet believes their poems will outlive them

every piece of furniture in my room is shaking its head

what's the difference between weeping alone & on camera

what's the gulf between an epitaph & an epic

what's a eulogy but a coin rising in the throat

eulogy from the greek means praise

praise from the latin means price

every public dirge is burning capital

every shirtless picture of him i keep is a small virgil

every hell i've traveled through is an expensive bird in my mouth

i was paid a thousand dollars for writing a poem about a dead man who hated me

i was paid & each dollar is a ghost haunting my wallet

i was paid & i am trading his body for bags of food

i am never more dangerous than inside

the arms of a man

who will die

before me

POEM ABOUT WATER

i get it. your body is blah blah blah percent water. oceans levitate, clouds urinate on the ground that grows our food. this is considered a miracle—this is a problem of language. i could go on for days with facts about the ocean and it will always sound like i'm talking about love. i could say: no man has ever seen its deepest trenches, we know less about its floor than the stars, if you go deep enough all your softest organs will be forced out of your mouth, you can be swallowed alive and no one will hear a sound. last summer three boys drowned in the sound and no one remembers their names, they came up white and soft as plastic grocery bags. i guess you could call that love. you'd be wrong.

IMPERMANENCE

sometimes i wonder what happens to people's hands when they disappear
in their pockets. of course, my rational brain knows they go on being hands
but there's still the question. i wonder if object permanence isn't the biggest
trick of them all, a scam, a way to ground the brain in its thin bath of liquid

don't worry, when you close your eyes the world goes on being the world, that dark
clearing cleaving open in your skull. don't worry, existence is a technology
like everything else, it can be broken & written down in an easier alphabet

then the thin membrane peels back & all your nerve endings start speaking
at once. i came out to my mother over text, each letter wept into place.
she erased that message & it never existed, my belief in objects disappearing.

every day the newspaper reads me death, every day bullets make their grand
entrances & exits, every day another friend takes his narrative in his own hands
& answers an old question. i'm left cursing paper, pulp emissary of loss,
messenger carved from the heart of a tree, each letter the bearer of bad tidings.

of course, my rational brain knows he is dead & will always be dead, but still
there is the question, language being a technology like everything else. i have
to wonder what happens if instead i read his story backwards, if it begins
with a flag at half mast making the noise a flag makes without wind & then
continues with his casket rising out of the ground. if it ends how all stories
end—an infant climbing into its mother, animals throwing themselves back
in the ocean

SERVICE

all roads lead to more roads. if you go
far enough you'll find a cathedral

or mcdonalds, either way, kneel
before god's gold archways

liquid pork + beef trimmings give
sovereignty to the meat

arch your back. men only kneel for one
of three reasons in rest-stop

bathrooms. beneath the synagogue
concrete. all religions borne

from the mouth of an exhaust pipe
or child king. as a boy i'd exhale smoke

toward heaven. the stars hanged dead
in their sky, tiny projectors

desperate archives. i'd lie naked
on my back below the red

traffic signal, my head an arrow
spinning in four directions

my pupil's great westward expansion
my blood, asphalt + fast in my veins

i watch him touch him   self over a screen
and pretend   it is my hands

how you pull a quiver   from an arrow.

he moans and i grow   jealous of satellites
their capacity for translation, to code his sound
in numbers   unbraid in speakers
lucky metal   audience of cables

i know the wireless signal is all around me,
that i'm drowning in his   unrendered noise.

how from a thousand miles away   i can dam
myself   with the light spilling from his hands.

what magic is this?   distance collapsed
into the length of a human breath. what witchcraft?

six years ago a bridge between us   collapsed
the interstate ate   thirteen people alive
asphalt spilling   like amputated hands
into the dark below.   what is love but a river
that exists to eat   all your excess concrete

appendages?   what is a voice but how it lands
wet in the body?   what is distance
but a place that can be reshaped through language?

how i emulate and pull a keyboard from the ashes.

how i gave him a river   and he became its king.

how any thing collapsed   can be rebuilt.
take our two heaving torsos   take them

how they fall like a bridge into the water

        how they rise up alone from the sweat.

BUTTHOLE

o putrid rose. o floral gift from some dead god
i buried alive only to excavate and find, still fresh.

o myriad sweet sounds i make with it: trumpet,
trombone, tornado, goblin. o second mouth

that gapes and swallows. o second mouth that hungers
for new tongue. o stomach that rests so far from

the colon but still calls him cousin. o come, o old
world magic, o small hungry prince.

how many octaves can you tuba? how many eloquent
speeches come right from the gut? what countless

phallic shapes have you named husband? what knuckle
tucked into you, a dyke holding up all this stale water.

sweet you who birthed iron when i took too many
women's multivitamins claiming there's no such thing

as gender. praise, how you expand and shrink like
a house's water pipes. praise, how when you bleed

you're always trying to tell me something. praise you,
tiny gymnast. beast with a breathing halo.

gold band that weds my strange body to this strange
strange earth.

BUTT PLUG

i paid extra
so you'd feel like skin

little engine
piece of paper with my name on it

ditched your hard rubber
ancestor for this silicone surrogate

have you ever seen
a rubber tree bled?

almost like a man
if you cut him

who knew petroleum
could be rearranged

to approximate
the feel of a body

little globe-shaped thing
you are the world

& what the world wishes
it could be

little artificial organ
all my training

could not prepare
me for

bless the tip & flange
unassuming gargantuan

blush, new husband
i carry in me all day

black synthetic abacus
solitary prayer bead

bless the phantom
you become

& the man who vanishes
when i'm done

bless the crow-slick
soaped washing

little coronation
the crown & the hole

little coroner opening
me to the unknown

APPLICATION

for a man who only loves the torso this must be heaven
holy, the photograph's mad beheading

lo, the framed anus
lo, the catfish
lo, the man posing with the cat on his chest

holy the shadow beard
holy the arm arched + tendered above the back
holy the trojan, the rightnow, the john23

o, the pictures we take of our simple sex
                                    lit + filtered cigarette
o, exile is a written language
                    + its digital equivalent is drooling

drive west a mile to be choked by a stranger
walk a block south to kneel on black + white linoleum
north is money + a mouth to empty inside

who better but all who want it, to host the host on their tongue

glory, the new houses i've become a part of
                    with a simple smear of semen below the couch
glory, the family portraits smiling as the husband drowns behind me
glory, the hole that opens + moves as i move

     sup / looking / you close
     you swallow / you travel / you host

of course the greek root of *icon* is a god
the plate of light i reach my hand through + feel it pulse
around my arm

a message from john23—313 ft. away
let me ruin your mouth + it's done. a man makes love
to his machine + then becomes one

PHONOMANIA

A HISTORY OF NOISE

polyphony, euphony, diapason, the oldest sound,
paramecium, parthenogenesis, to be torn in two,
to be made into, to grow legs, to be thrown up
on land, amphibious, bronchial, ligament, sound
carried like a filament, ligature, filigree, homo
habilis, homo sapiens, stone grunting into spark,
suit stitched from skins, the flicker of life forced
in a screaming belly, mesolithic, neolithic, cereal
crop planted in rows, metal molded into axe heads
and thrones, christ throwing tantrums at fig trees,
the first noise, capital, coffle, chattel, modernity,
same sound you dragged into the hospital with you,
your mother's face a whole note, your cradle song
a doctor's coat, echometry, homonymy, phonology.
dial-tone, desperation, aspiration, the depression
of computer keys, begging the stranger over,
concinnity, cacophony, on my knees, lips pressed
against the absence of your zipper, you in my mouth
like a new language, shape opening strange notes
in my neck, tongue i worked so hard to master,
but when you came inside me, my lord,
the sound you made.

GAY BOYS & THE BRIDGES
WHO LOVE THEM

it is not the fall, exactly. not the crash either, the swallow,
      the life flashing backwards behind the dark screen of the eyes,
         the water rising up to meet you.

no. it is not what drove your body here like a stolen car.
      why you abandoned it on this unreasonable ledge. not why
         you dove in, salt wind singing its perfect punctuation.

it is not the city stretching out before you waving
      its startled steel hands. it is not the last man who turned
         you down, or turned you out, or turned the camera on.

it is not the six seconds between here and impact,
      though each is its own poem. it is not how the body
         overflows like a damned river into its ocean,

the shopping mall of chemicals doing their patient
      and awful sorting. Not the suit of clothing you decided
         to die in, the wrinkled cotton jacket and its wet lineage.

The necktie and its flawless knot. it's not even the difference
      between being pushed and choosing to leave.

no. it is the wreckage
      spilling from the wreckage.

         it is the light
           throwing its last shade.

WILL

how deep am i indebted to the dead? i compile my list

of derelict crafts & acquisitions : begin with breath & end

with breath. all my calendars & colanders & cataclysms,

all my volumes of vonnegut & auden & baldwin, all my

gone men & all my felicific fictive children. to the dead

i leave every river delta left, what once fed the ocean fresh

water. to the dead i leave my letters for they were never mine

to begin with. i leave mine body—unless who outlasts me

decides otherwise : to make me a sky burial or diamond

or line of cocaine. to the living i leave, i leave the living

everything left. everyone i love is dying & i can't let this be

tragic : haunted hunted seraph, abandoned plate of deer ribs.

instead let every leaf of grass be my family's sick blood clean.

let me trust every writ letter is alive & liquid & will survive me.

acknowledgments

Apogee: Risk

The Beloit Poetry Journal: Ultrasound, Standards

Birdfeast: Impossible Drama

The Boiler: Silent Auction

Cherry Tree: Bridges

The Collagist: Will (The Fisherman)

Cortland Review: Politics of Elegy

Day One: Service

DIAGRAM: Bury (my father's biggest fear)

Drunken Boat: Gay Boys & the Bridges Who Love Them

Fourteen Hills: Buena Vista Park 2am

Fourway Review: Bildungsroman, I.35

Guernica: First Will & Testament

Gulf Coast: Weather Underground

Indiana Review: Impermanence

Iowa Review: Meat, Application

The Los Angeles Review: Kaddish

Meridian: Objectophile

The Minnesota Review: Synonyms for Raw

Muzzle Magazine: Butthole

The New England Review: Will (how deep am i)

Ninth Letter: Poem about Water

The Normal School: Naubade

PEN Poetry Series: I Want So Desperately to Be Finished with Desire

Phantom Limb: New God of an Antique War

Pleiades: Hydrophobia

Ploughshares: Controlled Burn

Poetry: Worry, Treyf

Prairie Schooner: Bury (i'm interested in death rituals), Missing Persons

Rhino: Essay on Crying in Public

Salt Hill: Phonomania

Southern Humanities Review: Butt Plug

TriQuarterly: MDMA

Washington Square Review: Pentimento, Surveillance

The following chapbooks and anthologies included poems from this
collection:

All the Rage (Sibling Rivalry Press): Synonyms for Raw

Best American Nonrequired Reading: Buena Vista Park 2AM

Best New Poets (2015): Gay Boys & the Bridges Who Love Them

Guide to Undressing Your Monsters (Button Poetry): Butthole

Reading Queer (Anhinga Press): Will, Objectophile, & Surveillance

Straight (Diode Editions): Kaddish & MDMA

▲

My deepest gratitude to so many people for being there for the many years
it took to make these poems. To everyone who taught me anything about
poetry & living, which are inseparable. To everyone who told me what wasn't
working with a hand to guide me toward what was. Special gratitude to
Hieu Minh Nguyen, Cameron Awkward-Rich, Franny Choi, Danez Smith,
Fatimah Asghar—y'all are giants. I'm so lucky to call you friends. Without y'all
I wouldn't be.

To my many teachers, mentors, companions, & friends: Kazim Ali,
D. A. Powell, Brigit Peegen Kelly, Dobby Gibson, Patricia Smith, Mona Webb,
Lisa Olstein, Elizabeth McCracken, Michael McGriff, Carrie Fountain,
Naomi Shihab-Nye, Jericho Brown, Alan Kaufman, Micheal Foulk, Kaveh
Akbar, Morgan Parker, Chen Chen, Bing Li, Jamila Woods, Charif Shanahan,
Meg Freitag, Baraka Noel, Dusty Rose, Dunce Apprentice, Tatyana Brown,
Jason Bayani, CalSlam, the Berkeley Slam, SpitShine, the New Sh!t Show,
Abbey Mei-Otis, F. T. Kola, Taya Kitaysky, Layne Ransom, Mark Cugini,
Paul Tran, Hanif Abdurraqib, Ariana Brown, Arati Warrior, Nic Alea, Seth
Moore, Gabriel Cortez, Natasha Huey. To Holli, Ben, Matt, Lauren, & my
grandparents—without y'all I wouldn't have language.

Much appreciation to the following institutions who've supported my
work: the Michener Center for Writers, Lambda Literary, the National
Endowment for the Arts, the Blue Mountain Center, the MacDowell Colony,
& the Round Top Poetry Festival. Thanks to Academy of American Poets for
choosing this book for the James Laughlin Award, I am so honored to be one
voice inside that long venerable conversation. Thanks to Suzanna Tamminen
& all the wonderful people at Wesleyan University Press. & lastly thank you for
taking your time to read this book, I cannot express what gratitude I feel for
this simple & sacred exchange.

notes

"Bildungsroman" uses a line from a Reddit thread.

"New God of an Antique War" borrows ideas from Cameron Awkward-Rich and Jane Hirshfield.

"Essay on Crying in Public" is in conversation with Cameron Awkward-Rich.

"Bridges" refers to the Golden Gate Bridge, which is the most popular suicide destination in the United States.

"I Want So Desperately to Be Finished with Desire" takes its title from a line in Aaron Smith's poem "Boston."

"First Will & Testament" is after a poem by Quan Barry.

"Surveillance" is composed of lines culled from news articles after Tyler Clementi's death.

"Politics of Elegy" is in conversation with Danez Smith.

"Impermanence" borrows an idea from Laura Eve Angle.

"Butt Plug" derives from a purchase in Austin, Texas.

"Phonomania" is after Reginald Dwayne Betts.

sam sax is a queer jewish writer and
educator. He's the author of *Madness* (Penguin,
2017), winner of the National Poetry Series,
and has received fellowships from the National
Endowment for the Arts, Lambda Literary,
and the MacDowell Colony. He's the two-time
Bay Area Grand Slam Champion and winner
of the Gulf Coast Prize, the Iowa Review Award,
and the American Literary Award. His poems
have appeared in *BuzzFeed*, *New York Times*, *Poetry*,
Tin House, and other journals. He's the poetry
editor at BOAAT Press.